SOMEHOW STILL WATERED WHEN IT WAS OVER

7

SOMEHOW STILL WATERED WHEN IT WAS OVER

poems

KEVIN DYER

Marrowstone Press

Somehow Still Watered When It Was Over © Kevin Dyer 2017
Marrowstone Press, ©*2017*
All rights Reserved

ISBN: 978-0-692-81441-3

Acknowledgements: 'Burmese Day for Night' first appeared in *Visions International*, Winter 2015

'Roan' appeared in *Josephine Quarterly*, Winter 2015

'The Darkest Apartment in Alphabet City' was published in *Two Cities Review*, Winter 2016

'Burmese Spice Market, Killing Floor,' was recently accepted by *Ink in Thirds*.

This book is dedicated to Peter Weltner,
whose ways of seeing, speaking, and writing about things
as they are, taught me how to live in the world.

TABLE OF CONTENTS

I

Riyadh, Empty Quarters, Red and Desert Seas

Riyadh, Letter from Khadija 1

Riyadh: Alluvial 2

Riyadh 3

Riyadh: Syrian Taxi Driver 4

Sudani, Woman Doctor 5

Empty Quarter#1: Sulayyil 6

Empty Quarter #2: Al-Ahsa 7

Empty Quarter # 3: Rub' Al Khali 8

Empty Quarter #4: Vertiginous 9

Red Sea 10

Red Sea #2: No One is Ever Missing 12

Red Sea #6: Safar, 1428 13

Red Sea # 7: English as a Foreign Language 14

Red Sea: Transit 16

Desert Sea 18

Desert Sea #5, Shamal 19

Desert Sea by Definition 20

Desert Sea Love Poem 21

II

Rivers of Grass, Staggered Birds, and Golden States

Sawgrass #1: Inside, Looking Out 25

Sawgrass #2: Disappearance 26

Sawgrass #3: In Florida, All Birds Are Winter Birds 27

Sawgrass #4: December Swale 28

Sawgrass #5: December, Drifter 29

American River 30

Darn That Dream 31

Black Spring 32

Lullaby 33

Quarry 34

Quarry 2 35

Marina 36

Golden State 37

Golden State: Anatomy of Love 38

Golden State: The Potential in The Rough (Cocteau) 40

Golden State: Soft Opening 40

III

Burma, Before the Name Change

Mission of Burma 45

Burma, Pure Landscape 46

Burmese Spice Market, Killing Floor 47

Burma, or Colonialism Gone Wrong 48

Burmese Day #2 49

Burmese Elegy 50

Burmese Day For Night 51

Burmese Journalist 52

IV

Four Mimosas, Earthly Matters Mimosa
#1: This Undoing 55

Mimosa #2: The Left, The Leaving 56

Mimosa #3: Gut-Spilling 58

Mimosa #4: Invasive Species 59

Blind Squirrel 60

Gone To Seed 61

The Unraveling 62

Flat Earth 63

Can You Ever Be Loved Long Enough? 64

Roan 65

Public Authority 66

Hearing Voices 67

Along The Way 68

Sunday, or Something Mapped 69

Mr. Robinson Learns To Separate #1 70

Mr. Robinson Learns To Separate #2 72

How to Listen 74

How to Listen #2 75

Nature, Terror 76

The Darkest Apartment in Alphabet City 77

I
Riyadh, Empty Quarters, Red and Desert Seas

Riyadh, Letter from Khadijah

The school for girls starts early,
the sun just there–
little light beyond the headlights as
we avoid the new ring-road to skirt the traffic.
The world kohl-black, compulsory,
the driver turns to tell me
there's no turning back from what
the police set up–
but not to worry–it's only for those without the right papers,
night and day laborers who send away
everything they make–never allowed to go home
until they're herded, packed, sent away
so they can't come back.
Only you can choose, secretary or nurse, clerk in
a shop, just for girls;
dark against the daylight,
the faint sun a guide to brightness.
The weather turns, and I do too,
away from the car into the concrete yard.
I take it
as it comes,
new rain falls:
washing myself of myself,
school girl collected
behind the school walls.

Riyadh: Alluvial

Can you fathom the river's reach, skimming the surface, beyond the depths
as an indweller would?
Off-book, no kind comfort
in currents as they winnow away
whatever takes
between the banks
they daily make, unmake. Impossible
to branch off,
what's left
of love,
a kind of chaff.

Riyadh

Rain fell over
the city for the first time since you arrived.
It left the world–
in your blood–
the bone of something
beneath a knee-high palm. A mortal wound however you take it;
The sky opened up:
a surgical strike, or
a way of seeing,
trying to keep out–terrifying, even though you never said that.

Riyadh: Syrian Taxi Driver

The dust, risen up–
a glance backward is all
you can gather. Your eyes are glass.
An engine run roughshod–
a trail of oil,
or a name for yourself.
A cricket match
in a rock-strewn field. Flagged down,
bodies pouring over fences
as the wind picks up–
blinding everyone, for a moment–
and anyone can be anybody, in full pursuit of a ball across the dirt,
sidestepping stones,
flying over magnificent holes
that hold the arc of an afternoon
were you to land there
brittle in your bones,
from another age.
So many children
gather there
until the call to prayer
takes what is left of mid-air,
and everyone just disappears.

Sudani, Woman Doctor

By late afternoon, few shadows
show up that fell
mid-morning.

Depending on the door,
no river's edge–
like an afterthought, wedged in–
the light, see-through–

a window where
the roof had been;

sand, stone,
the anteroom walled-in, which
is your thinking.

Empty Quarter#1: Sulayyil

The sands are rarely level—though lone—
they swell and fall, softly carved
in sinuous forms
that somehow, at some point, stop.

Though that is inaccurate. Take me to the dark,
and we can feel the nothing that remains
as it unsettles underfoot. In the distance,
there is further distance. Stand there long enough,
and you will understand just what
that sinking feeling is.

You told me I was far away. I think that was meant as metaphor.
But I am, and will be, and as the horizon thins at
the disappearance of the sun, don't look.

Empty Quarter #2: Al-Ahsa

The heat is the least of it.
As ever, whatever swells gets the most
attention. I tried to be the squeaky wheel,
but never quite got the grease.

The dunes rise without a sound. You might hear
sand as it splays in heavy wind against
your window, but that is going nowhere—
you will find it in thin layers across the house,
hardly of any import. Vacuum.
Get the broom.

Yet as the road unwinds, and
the dunes slant side by side,
unabridged, you will feel
a certain splendor in the manner
of their making. I'd stake
everything on this.

You could imagine a ship, a ferry,
shepherding us across with great intensity,
to a world—neither barren nor ravaged—
no wasteland—where the sun, before it ever
falls, inoculates the moon, and we settle
in a darkness beyond all wandering.

Empty Quarter # 3: Rub' Al Khali

I was unshriven early on.
It was surely a crooked thing,
pilloried by the most recidivist of
memories.

It takes a soiled priest to know one,
or a fellow traveler on an unravelling mountain pass,
knowing the woman across the aisle is praying the bus
will breach the cliff-edge, at last.

The *Empty Quarter* is no metaphor.
It is pure desert, nothing more.
Its borders—shift—so that it is
never mapped with any accuracy.

It is only inhospitable to man,
its careless body spans unalloyed
to any industry—and it is this we will remember—
that to be forgiven for any past transgression
is here—the sand in the wind-swirl, filling
your eyes, stinging your skin—
until we can begin again—half-covered by the dunes.

Empty Quarter #4: Vertiginous

If today were terminal,
and under strict conditions of the
conditional, it is—I would sit
on the couch and watch *Vertigo*
until the sand ran out.

In daily life, there is rarely, if ever, dénouement,
just rising and falling action, and if we address the end of
every act, catastrophe. There is sand along the windowsill.
It sits in corrugated waves, in wavering bits of sunlight.

Still, in 1958, I was nothing. I couldn't even have been in
love with Kim Novak, or wished that Jimmy Stewart would let me
sublet his apartment on Russian Hill. Yet I find myself there.
I know it's a script. And how it was made.
That changes nothing.

Today, when I briefly stepped outside, the world
was wide and none of it seemed round. Sand swept itself across
the ground in slim, granular creeks, or rivulets. I wasn't sure.

I bask in the end. The sand
wends its way along no particular path. Through time, men have made use of
it for wearing away whatever was.

Red Sea

Last night the Red Sea swallowed the sun.
There were families spread across
the sand to watch it go.
Like many things, it
was deceiving
and has happened before.

You could be forgiven
for thinking rain, given
the way the sky darkened
and the wind came
up. To no avail.

The sea stays alive at night.
You might not know, under
all that darkness.
The waves are inexhaustible—
throwing themselves against the seawalls,
even when you're not there.
Though the waterfront is tired.
You can just tell.

Listen, since there's little in the way
of time. The children use
the sand for building. You know
this creates a network
of dashed expectations,
but you keep quiet.

Save that old saw about
what you see in
a grain of sand. We were
bereft enough. Under the weather, the world
folding up in a wave.

Red Sea #2: No One is Ever Missing

Around the curve the headlights
froze a man standing near the sea
in a dirty thobe–
the streetlight splintered up the road in heavy fog.

At the base, soldiers wander around in fatigues. The
empty football stadium
holds the only field of grass the city has.
You can feel the Red Sea rising up outside the glass.

By mid-morning, the fog burns away; light falls across
the spent missiles on the parade grounds.
There is something like music, and men marching
in nothing like straight lines.

In class the other day
we studied irregular verbs.
A student asked me the past of dead.
Because my parents, he said.

It's an adjective not a verb, I had to say,
so it stays the same and doesn't change.

Red Sea #6: Safar, 1428

I drive to work
and the moon is out, still full.
The road unwinds along
the sea. People stand
next to their cars, looking out.
At the waves, I guess,
though they must be hard to see.
The women are covered
in black in the darkness.

There are no women where I work.
They're not allowed.

A kid told me my name means
burial shroud in Arabic.
The sky is grey ash
with light behind.
Soldiers line the parade ground,
the clouds in strange formations.

On Friday, the holy day,
people will be executed in the public square.
Others will have a hand or a limb removed.
I've never seen, though I hear
locals take their children there.

In the pitch black morning, the call to prayer
fills in the air between one mosque
and another, then another, until that's
all there is.

Red Sea # 7: English as a Foreign Language

The students sit, taking a test.
There's a dead cat outside the class.

The air conditioners on high.
I don't know why they're here, learning English.
They speak one language already.
It works fine.

They're all older, married.
I'm sure each with only one wife since it's too expensive
anymore to keep
two or three, they tell me.
My wife stays inside.
She's not allowed to drive.

Meanwhile, the students fill in bubbles and blanks.
There's not much of the cat left.
It's flat and hard.

When the students get home,
perhaps their wives ask them what
they've done, how they spent
their day.
What they learned.
Maybe they don't say anything.

The test is over.
The students file out,
talking quietly in Arabic,
separating into different cars.
Tomorrow is Thursday;
it's the weekend.

There are a few cats around,
thin and dirty, scavenging for food,
running from people.

It's not too hot yet
but you can tell
they won't make it to summer.

Red Sea: Transit

A grey day in the city of
lights,
though it has little to do
with Paris—a terminal at
the airport's edge.

There are no discernible
clouds,
just an all-over cover, and
a wind
that unstifles the trees.

You want something,
that unasked for movement
that comes just in time,
when your life and all that
is arrives.

Fuck it
escapes your mouth
too loud,
and people
at the other table turn
and turn around—

back to smoking,
to the window
where the world is—

a bit of brightness
inside the grey,
the planes in a line
and the wind won't die.

Desert Sea

Fleshed-out, broke the skin,
drawn in by what you knew by then
had lowered your threshold
    for pain.

The waves, in heavy wind–
your heart still in you–
yet few could argue
    against the violence

plastered across the sea-wall,
such a natural disaster.
Time doesn't move
    though it moves right

through you. Now they've torn down
the old billboard
the tattered ad for nothing new
    that daily saved me.

Desert Sea #5, Shamal

Outside the coffee shop, birds in the dirt,
a cat's tail half-shorn off. A story of your
life—come back—without hope,
or fear, tenderness in some
kind of contrast.

When despair strikes out, I try be sensible,
though really, the light dies as it rises
when you half-expect it to stick around.
Over time, reconciliation proves
a nasty habit to get into, favoring, as it does,

what you recollected over what
burned as it went down.
That silent town, save the few stragglers
who couldn't keep it shut
before everything went.

When you do go back,
don't forget to tell anyone who will listen
about the weather that day, how the wind
blew everything loose across the dirt courtyard
but the birdsong, the cat trapped between cars.

Desert Sea by Definition

Night has clearly fallen.
How long does it last–trying
to bridge a distance which simply
spreads, stretched thin

between either end?
I never knew how it went with you.
All that ocean over the earth,
a body in fluid motion,

immersed in itself.
Everything is invented,
and the urge to return to
is, more aptly, to revert–

a northern desert at night,
barren rock fields–
neither water nor snow,
and incredibly cold.

Desert Sea Love Poem

The body of a bird–
sideways, blown stiff.
A clot of feathers,
weather-shift,
wind-chill

down the narrow corridor.
Play it where it lands;
a warm body,
bird-feathered,
is too much to ask for.

So much at a glance:
a man in a wheelchair—
and another man
leaning in–
feeding him by hand.

II

Rivers of Grass, Staggered Birds, and Golden States

Sawgrass #1: Inside, Looking Out

A slaughter house in the center
of a southern, river-side city–
It wreaks havoc, quietly.
No animals, or signs,
for miles outside.

At times it's more than enough
to feel upside down, or underwater, and the line every-
one, one day,
has to stand in–winds and winds around,
the end–
as if a cloud were
the only thing that could hold anything.

I woke to darkness–
everyone immersed in talk
about draining the swamp–
incapable of seeing
the permanent catastrophe
that took root there,
no shelter from the outside wind.

I looked for you in the river of grass, the fresh-water
 marsh.
And found only a wetland
shaped by water and fire,
ferns–climbing
up the canopy
making certain every
salt-water tree
would go up in
an instant–a lightning strike–
keeping everything that dies there
water-tight.

Sawgrass #2: Disappearance

Even the smallest creatures
arrive fully formed.
Perfect ribcage–
heart and lungs,
life strung between
the veins like thin wire.

There is a world that exists only
some depth beneath the water–
no one's fault–
but native bladder-wort that feeds
the unseen and see-through is no
water-lily, choking the
estuary. Sawgrass burns
and throws down roots
above it all.
I would like to think
that about you, too.

Alligators carve out holes
they later come back to sink into.
Saw palmettos rake the sky,
rookeries for birds.

Somehow, for some time, sustained
by the atmosphere–water sucked up
through the trees--seems only to carry on and upward–
that disappearance we can
never get ahold of--
wait for the alligator-prey–
the breath that won't catch,
hidden in leaves.

Sawgrass #3: In Florida, All Birds Are Winter Birds

The clouds darken,
separate–indiscriminate
shapes along the skyline.

Impossible to map
the gradients of grief–
the steep drop-off
beneath the water-line
gives way to where the coral beds
disappear, and the immense gulf
carved out along the sea-floor
is suddenly, here.

You stare out.
The cantilevered bridge;
mangroves of regret.
And in the skeletal rigging
of the ship at harbor,
drying their wings–
little grey herons
sandhill cranes–
snowy egret
after egret.

.

Sawgrass #4: December Swale

The process
of elimination—what
life—the trail through
the trees
led us to believe.

The story they told—
sea-salt marsh,
water-swept edge—
brought us back to earth
while having none of it.
It had the air of
the empty—
the sun, without reflecting—
left the rest for last.

The old ways of doing things—
tarred-and-feathered, drag
the river—better left
to a world where it's
hard to demarcate where
the shore-bird stops and
the dwindling flock begins;

a nest built,
nothingness
woven in—

attenuated longing, abbreviated wind.

.

Sawgrass #5: December, Drifter

The water, whipped
into wave-lengths, speaks–
aftermath in the air–
wild ginger folded under,
moss hung up in the trees.

If inherent in everything
is a matter of degrees,
then winter here
wants for nothing.
Palm trees fall across the roadway in
the accelerated, afternoon wind–
splintered fronds,
resembling leaves.

All I ever wanted was
to bifurcate-–split
and fall away
where I might never
hear you–voices
collect and replicate, yet
all that resounds
is a singular bird call
under the boardwalk,
down by the sea.

Foam laps the shore-line.
Pressure, ever-exerted,
exists to convince you of something.
The waves tumble to sea-level, re-create
and rise–
pulled under,
crest after crest
of the breakers.

American River

Off-white birds
stagger along the bank, looking
immersed in whatever you thought
they were.

It's not for me to know
how soon
all of this will be the end of you.
The river is heartless.

It collects at the confluence,
unnamed, another river
that takes what can't stay,
and carries it away from you forever.

Darn That Dream

Morning lights
the river slowly
through the shallows,
the still rock,
half-shadow.

Little trace of the Romans
save the aqueduct, water
unwinding through the valley,
emptied into acre after acre, flat,
scorched fields.

Pulled by gravity.
A Northern California boyhood dream,
scores of orange trees
along the road,
endless almond groves.

Today the sign says extreme fire danger.
Up the hill high above
the ranger
station, four planes with little air between them
here and gone, locked in formation.

Black Spring

Black spring
butterflies, vultures
in the wind, silently arc
above the fire
break. A tree recently fallen,
roots up.

No murder mystery.
In the gulag, on Solovetsky,
they tied prisoners to a post
in a mosquito swarm.
Pushed others down
flights of endless
wooden stairs.

Today
I'll take
my sorrow
to go.
A pair of geese call through
the canyon–

flying upriver, reversing
the current–
where the river narrows and slows,
a man wading in,
panning for gold.

Lullaby

The river stills,
clear where the bend is.
Sun sidles up the hillside,
light and dark.

Oh, make of me a riverbed,
laid open, spread wide,
not so much in licentious-
ness
as regard

for whatever
outweighed the river.
Sedimentary.
I hope

you can take me
like this.
There's no other way
left.

Quarry

Two days ago
the river ran low–
up against boulders,
metamorphic rock.
Once deeply buried.

Trains came and went
across the confluence,
quarried limestone, granite–
The tracks pulled up
for scrap when the war hit.

Quarry 2

Morning, light
wind in the trees.
Years back, what

they mined
was the heart
of the matter,

quarried scars
up the ridge-line,
deep in the gorge.

What doesn't last
stays with you.
The train takes its time

at night, passing by.
Not that;
the dark sound of it.

Marina

Redwing blackbird
out of the blue,
on a branch.

The garden mostly barren,
a few leaves,
pale yellow, newly green.

From this height
the river is aquamarine
all the way

through, diffused
between sand and clay.
What is left

of that gift?
A gemstone for protection, safe voyage,
water to the sea.

Golden State

On the sun deck, out back,
a man fingers the air
where his ear was,
and peers across the spreading waves
that shift from white to grey
while the shore birds lift, and linger,
above the shallow forms in the wake.

Under the bridge there's a Ferris wheel
spinning slow turns, a long-ago carnival
of distance and lights. Soon
it will be early when the darkness
comes, and the pink stain of sky
quickly drips beneath the eye,
as the day edges out around
the island, the trees.

It all slows down.
This water covers the earth.
There's a man–
his ears missing, his nose gone,
making circles with his hand
in the twilight air,
black-lifting this halo
of night, a body of water
beyond the spray.

Golden State: Anatomy of Love

Tonight the artificial light
is clearly driven by the beginning—
the furnace blast, carbon
caught fire, metals, molten
and poured into iron ore—
conflagration at the essential core.

It was easy before.
The simple divide between day and
night, coupling in heat on top of
the wild earth, under the dome of sky
while seeds fell from the new trees:
we lay across the green world
in the fragrant grass.
And it was good.

And when did love begin?
On that first day, delivered from the dust, inhaled
at one with the breath of life?
No matter.
At any rate, it spread.

Until the moment of exposure at the high altar
with the plunge into the chest
and the heart pulled, held skyward, beating:
the locus of love for all to see.

And now, songs of loss
leak across the face of each and every one,
the sheets of music all the same
save the nightly notations of empty bars
filled with the sound of leaving—
the endless echo in the inner ear
of a dead-bolt thrown behind a door.

Were the gods pleased, appeased
by the offerings? No telling.
How I must seem, seen from the heavens:
love-struck, dumb-founded.
Still, perhaps for a moment
they have seen me—
freshly-fractured, luminous in the light,
and they cannot turn away—
agog for once in their never-ending lives,
startled at my luster.

Golden State: The Potential in The Rough (Cocteau)

The sun, such a constant—would
disappear if you let it. But that—
a rip-current, when the surf is rough—
leaves you locked in at wave-height before
breaking, just as the light lets go of a shimmer across the water.

Isn't it lovely, all that surface, caught up
in an image? Even birds would be drawn to it,
diving under for what might be found there.
Yet remember, as a swimmer, the shore-line
fading—it's not the pulling under, but being
carried away that matters.

Wave after wave batters the beach, undermining the edge
where the houses are. They have nothing to say—even with so
much to see—not architectural integrity, though everyone
on the sun deck basks in the afternoon
with alacrity, torso after torso.

You bowled me over, really, with all
that talk about what you meant,
though that was not what you said. That's standard
anymore—I know—I get it—you
had the hull of the argument—my expression—
and whatever seemed more like a laceration
was lessened by the birds in the backyard, in the trees,
fragmentary songs as the morning said so.

The details—cells, uncontrollably dividing—
eventually knock us out. Washing away
is all you can wish for—the houses—
for all they're worth, impediments
collapsing, in a froth that came
and never went.

Golden State: Soft Opening

At the outer edge of Shreveport–
birds on a distant wire.
There is no wind. They remain unswayed.

They appear painted, discrete marks of darkness
in the foreground. It would be easy to invest them with–
something–
a way to mark the end of a time when you
somehow survived–but that would
suggest they had something to say
about a world in which they have no investment,
being birds.

So let them stay there, birds on a distant wire,
the day dying behind them,
the sun nothing much–
for as long as today is
not yet night
you might arrive
as a fragment
from a lost language newly-deciphered,
unearthed in
mid-air.

III
Burma, Before the Name Change

Mission of Burma

Tin-roof rust,
angled
where the water falls–

grey-green moss coats
the brick
of every building
built
before you were born.

In the street,
beneath the edifice
of The *Government Telegraph Office*

feathered hens dangle
from the back of a bicycle

and the power goes out.

Burma, Pure Landscape

Sparse at first,
clouds re-gather in
a grey huff above the river,
dank even in daylight.

What washes up on the banks
tells you everything
you need to know
about how a country
measures low and high tides,
or if it's worthwhile,
what with all that untenable
cardboard and scrap metal

cobbled together by people living
up and down
the water-line.
You're not the first.
For years,
one cantilevered bridge existed
across the *Irrawaddy*
before the British took it out.

Burmese Spice Market, Killing Floor

Downtown, across the street
from the Hindu temple
the spice market abuts
the abattoir, where, once
domesticated, then gutted, their blood runs down
the concrete gutters.

I have had no one's hands
on me in forever,
and if I go this way—
in yet another sodden
southeast Asian city—
the sky gone grey,

dragonflies swarming
in broken arcs
above the broad-leaf trees—
there'll be little left.
So today I'll take this
walking steady, and slow,

in the flow of human traffic,
for the moment,
current.

Burma, or Colonialism Gone Wrong

The sky today, a collection
of clouds above
the power poles,
old, electrified wire
unwound across the city.

It's clear
that we're not from here,
though there's nowhere
else for now, save a slow-motion
rewind of a time of us—then,
a flock of grey birds
in the heart of the wind.

Someday we'll be skeletal
all over again,
and the new day
will be nothing more
than a wave of light
that pours
right through us.

Burmese Day #2

Pale song-birds
nest under the eaves,
light green this side of the rain.

It's no longer possible
to ignore the river,
the flooded pagoda—

a stroke of luck
as the stupa lit up,
struck gold
when the rain went.

Burmese Elegy

The skyline seems sculpted
from tossed-off things, a scrapped
collection with no spring wall of
leafy greens
for protection.
Winter light
continually fractures.

Ragged branches claw at nothing without moving.
In Rangoon I saw
a black snake longer than I am
slide across the side street where I lived and sink
back into the dark stream
that ran between the houses.

The kids ask me all kinds
of unforeseeable questions:
Do you like John Denver?
You got beat when you were little? I have to say yes,
not just because it's all true,

but for the fact that
if you say no it's the end of any kind of magical
thinking
for everyone,
all over.

Burmese Day for Night

For everyone I know,
it's 3 in the morning
when, for me, it's
strangely 4:30
in the afternoon.

It's a time I don't know
how to fill. There's no one
there, in the aether
or otherwise, and what
I have to say, then,
dissipates as the never-ending

rain comes on.
But oh, if you were there
when I needed you,
I could talk about the mud
that clings to everything
and how the people are
ground down in ways

which are hard to recognize,
at first. But that comes later.
Across from my house
they have Christmas lights inside,
flashing through
the night at the onset of September,
but that is something for
another time, when I can reach you.

Burmese Journalist

They found you
where they'd left

you, though it
took some time

for someone else
to point that out
without admitting anything.
Underneath, missing teeth,

cheekbones crushed, head
caved in, though there were five
further bullets which probably
weren't called for.

The sun ekes out
faint light where the clouds fade
into the sky's margins.

They say
the rainy season comes to an end.
But it never does,
for the rain that fell, running in errant streams

over everything
collects in shallow plots
beneath the earth
and never disappears.

IV
Four Mimosas, Earthly Matters

Mimosa #1: This Undoing

By silk degrees,
we ended up, where most
would have it—in the creek, the
river—and if you push it, the sea.

That was what I meant by
not stopping, and saying nothing.
I mean really, even
weeds flower,
before the early evening mower
and the bees, germinating on the wing,
don't suspect
conspiracy or anything.

And there you are, a
downward arc into
today's darkness.
I try to keep the
summer song, but the singer,
it seems, died not too
long ago, despite
the clement weather.

What is left to do in this undoing?
Crying out is one way to go,
but your silent breaking
is what keeps the less-deciduous
at bay.

Bamboo, when
it freezes, or gives way,
cracks with alarm to
those near—who can hear it—
spent—
dry bone the
only referent.

Mimosa #2: The Left, The Leaving

The innate
drive to delineate
shade cuts across—
indeed abuts—the basic
fact of the season—
whichever one you've chosen.

Of the many things I needed to be told,
that a cemetery is not a
multi-purpose facility
was yet another. Face down, I
tried to find the secret life
distilled from underground,
but found my breath too shallow
to get at it.
Impenetrable,
what comes after.

Making a wrong turn,
I passed a playground, the swing set full,
four girls back and forth,
high in the air— their little legs
almost eclipsing the branches—
the trees were basking in it, waving
in the foreground.
Some things are a flying buttress
for the heart—Chartres, stained windows, undestroyed
along the river, the red birds
lifted by the slightest
summer wind.

Mimosa tree, you have left me,
but that was not your doing.
Still, I have your image
extant in that spot in
my mind shaded
by your constant canopy—though now,
scoured clean by fractious autumn light—
I will expect your return much later
in the year—
though I can't promise to
be here—just a platform, a train—
a figure smeared and framed
against the night.

Mimosa #3: Gut-Spilling

Oh, mimosa—it's pathetic—
however accurate—I logged
so many hours in your presence
I became completely arboreal—
alternately stiff and pliant, bifurcated
in places, needing rain—
bending in the wind when it seemed right.
I loved that aspect—
being at your best just standing in one place.

I could never, however,
get the hang of attracting birds
to my leafless branches—I must have
seemed too unstable for nesting.
And soon, it became apparent I
was not much longer able—
the thunder and lightning
rewired my ambulatory instincts—
and so stiffly, I shuffled back in.

Mimosa, before I lamented
the fact of your leaving—but really,
I dissolved far earlier than you in the
broad light of day—I was nowhere—and I know,
if you had the ability, you would have renounced
me there and then.

But by that time I was far—gone—
now a deer in his
wild mind—on the run—who threw his full body
against the side of a moving
car—with great speed if not skill—
or perhaps—if half of the game
is just to
be killed.

Mimosa #4: Invasive Species

You were there,
mimosa tree, in that summer onslaught—when
there weren't—when I needed—hotly flowered
you fanned out across
the gravel drive.

That talk turned to an invasive species
was to be expected.
Duly inspected, the dogwood was pronounced
dying at the scene in your shadow.
Thus the neighbors
cut you back somewhere across the
property line.
It must have been
too much for them, especially
the children, to see us so close.

Woe was I those overheated afternoons.
Though still, you kept me, despite
my inability to understand the root
of anything.
And now, in that all-subsuming, glacial shift
the sun stays low
and your spent seeds fall in the culvert
where no one goes.

There is little left.
Save something in the frenetic
twitching of the grey squirrel's tale
astride your trunk, upside down:
Today, crack the exposed bone of the branches;
tomorrow, gutter and scrape
the marrow.

Blind Squirrel

Winter comes.
And stays. It's always enough.
The wind that wreaks
Small havoc in the leaves
that are already dead.

If I had a grandfather he
would tell a story that would help
us get through all this.
But he died, you see, so far back
and never had much of anything
to say to anybody, anyway.
He used to listen to a transistor radio for company.

So very few things help,
rarely people. I met a blind squirrel once
in Central Park when I wanted to die,
and he did something in the nimble way he took
the peanuts from my invisible hand with his strange fingers.

One day I will walk into the park to find him
but he will be gone. Squirrels don't live very long.
People do—and something about that will keep things raw.

I'd rather have a blind squirrel as a lifelong friend
who knows that winter is immanent, and we
are inured from none of it,
and will always take so gracefully what you have
and disappear into the trees,
knowing, in his belly, you'll come back.

Gone to Seed

Today, mid-freeway,
I want a bumper sticker
that says

the bigger the truck
the smaller the cock
though that would only

mean, like
them, I protest
too much.

Such a day,
things passing I'll never get,
like string theory or

miniature golf.
I'm better at nothing.
Sitting, legs on a chair.

An afternoon
in sunlight,
simply there.

The Unraveling

Startled,
the small birds scattershot
from the road-side trees–
somehow re-gather, a dark
recollection given flight.

Words thrown up, as if,
protection from a summer fog.
Long, the wayward–the torn fabric
pulled up sharp.
Not a word for the
way it went.

Still, wouldn't it be something,
jolted out of life, a pre-existing
condition, to wordlessly gather
together,
the sun lighting up the water–
shot through a bank of clouds
deliberately–

the rent of what was
left of us
slowed down enough
so everyone could see.

Flat Earth

The storm lashes in–
rain in rivulets down windows,
hard to see,
where the street begins, the slanted building
that always needs renting–
what the sea leaves,
the shore-walls where it rose up, over:
a broken-down arrangement of everything
we've ever made.

The old maps, cloven cartographies
of what might have been,
there, across the surface of this
and every other body:
an illuminated monster, destined to sink ships,
pulling everything asunder
with great velocity, casually
dashed across a crook of rocks,
the man-made ships at harbor.

Can You Ever be Loved Long Enough?

The sky finishes a
flattened grey, interspersed, thin red flecks or interstellar
paper cuts,
a yellowing moon stuck
in the midst.

Each night, despite the drought
desiccating every other body of water,
the river inside you rises up, rushing into and through
anything you can think of.

The air between bones.
First there were stairs,
then outside escalators,
which never move with no one there this time of year.

Winter daffodils spring up through
hoary grass.
Crows in the live oak outside the window.
The last place you'll ever look.

Roan

Through and through,
thought that—roan
horses, other fenced-in animals
that never go grey,
age in any way you can readily see.

Not that I ever forgot—
but whatever you loved
was just one way from here—
in response to an intended wound,
the softest, or the hardest hit, move
in a way that's painful to recognize.

An image in steady decline—
stippled blood across the forehead,
almost a straight line.

Public Authority

Cherry blossoms line the highway,
in the foreground
a bird
you'll never know,
hint of a song escaped,

scraped from those scantily-clad branches.
What if you had
instead of a target,
a sign someone stuck on your back
that said

Whatever happens, I'm always here?
What you might find
if you could scrape through the sky–
that time does not exist
until that's all there is.

Today, took a calculated risk–
shook out a fistful
of blueberries
for the birds.

Hearing Voices

A web, woven
before you could awaken

bright filaments
in the wind,
a spiral the heart
could never hold.

There was a day when
music escaped your mouth,

the song of
how narrow
the world is even
with us in it,

all that talk about spinning
around something that never moves,

like you were when you were little
and no one said or heard a word.
What does anyone want?
It seems more than all of us could ever handle.

Hummingbirds, smaller and more alive
than you could ever be–

in the summer trees
mock apples
fall in the dry grass

somehow still
watered when it was over.

Along The Way

The tree leans
away from the wind,
an invisible, permanent path.

I have been gone
forever, the years condensed
into something deceptively simple,

the past.
In the garden,
yellow blooms.

The day is at the door.
You can't help
but walk right into it.

Sunday, or Something Mapped

Gunmetal sky,
slate if that sounds right,
all afternoon
until night came. What if you were
an arrow, let go from someone's bowstring,
updrafts of air as you went,
streams of wind right through you?

On most maps you could
figure out where you were heading.
At any rate, no one would ever
know if you fled that way,
across and over the
digital hills, swiftly fording
man-made rivers.

In dreams, there is always someone
who doesn't fit the narrative,
who calls out
your name in
the coming dark,
which is always
yours.

Mr. Robinson Learns To Separate #1

It starts
in the morning–the sun–
unable to shed
light on much of anything–
as if it weren't already of
the aether,
far beyond the earth,
setting and re-setting itself on fire.

So much of life is merely self-reflexive–
I feed myself (sporadically, at uneven intervals)
and late at night
I think (myself)
into the rocky shallows of
the dark lake
some exits up the interstate.
Thus to
lacerate
(infinitive)
is just that,
ongoing, too deep to bleed,
a series of self-induced
wounds no one would notice,
or care to see.

The grim
reality is the clarity
exhumed from a body
(just beneath
the last, cracked right rib)
as it bolts upright
at nothing there–
and later,
even with the light on–
still nothing,
nothing still.

Mr. Robinson Learns To Separate #2

Unasked, the sun
came through the glass,
splitting the room. Each branch
bifurcated the broken fence—
which could stop at nothing.

By early afternoon,
I can't get my head around anything.
The birds must be dying of thirst—
though at least they keep quiet.
There must be a limit to this.

I was struck by insufficient things—
You wouldn't believe me if I told you—
suffice to say I left most of what remained
in the scattered hands of a neighbor and
god
knows what he did. Though his wife
left some time back, taking
most of everything.

It falls to me to
post the upshot of what
never was. It was ample,
owing more to the spoor
that leaked through the woods
where I followed, ready to find
whatever was.
Much to what I first believed
to be relief—
the trail forked—
later proved either way was incorrect,
and was left uncollected at an intersection

of flowering weeds.
I can't completely recall
but the sun, at some point, fell.
Though we know it never went anywhere.
The evening wind picked up, an
oceanic swell through the skittering, serrated leaves,
laying waste to the
last of the summer trees.

How to Listen

The leaves–unspoken things–
have a way of weaving in
before you can
say anything.

What gets
away, after all, is easy.
As it turns out–
you could have stayed, looked away,
and never have known.

The sky, at its height,
is uneventful.
If only you could
dog-ear those days

when you were there
and nowhere—
that sun just fading, a few words woven in,
the trees, falling where the moss fell first,

just for you to hear
one after another
in the heart of
your forest.

How to Listen #2

The rain comes down,
the palms folding in,
sharper leaves in
the summer wind.

It's a terror
that we dream of, then live,
disembodied voice after voice
given free reign,
self-replicating
stains all the way.

It's hard to watch the waves
of your world fall
without contention,
one after another, knocked
behind the knees as
the pier goes quiet;

It's not as if no one cares--
they just have to figure out how, then can't, and
when you wake in the morning
or on an early afternoon
it's not merely the weather
and what that might engender,

but the definition of love
as it folds in,
and the wind that comes,
unasked for, again—that sheer velocity,
blown through your shades.

Nature, Terror

Cows, winter calves
mill about. Horses
blanketed in the barn.

Not tragic so much as
commonplace. A plane in the air.
What we weather.

Some time later
someone will take
the hand away

from your face,
then the other hand.
Think of that

the next time something
happens you could never imagine
when you can't hold your face in your hands.

The Darkest Apartment in Alphabet City

Insofar as the light finds
its way fragmented,
the brick walls retain
the thin welt
of the days
that in theory, arrive.

In the square the guide
on the walking tour says
this is the place where once
when he means
time is gauged
in terms of erosion,
the cracking monuments
in mid-air,
the archives of the heart
lodged in a building no longer there.

In the story of the bird
trapped in a bright kitchen
all that is utterable
is the sound of impact—
a brief thud
and a new vision
of a world through glass
and the blur thereafter
deeply grafted.

An accidental clarity,
like the day I shot the background
with you walking up Christopher Street,
as though you lived there,
or were leaving.

Kevin Dyer received an MA in literature from San Francisco State University. A native Californian, he has spent most of his post-collegiate life living and working inside and outside of the United States—New York, Florida, North Carolina, Micronesia, Indonesia, Myanmar, Saudi Arabia, and Oman.

This is his first book.

www.ingramcontent.com/pod-product-compliance
Lightning Source LLC
Chambersburg PA
CBHW032046290426
44110CB00012B/982